Waiting
Laughters

(a long song in many voices)

Niyi Osundare

© Niyi Osundare 1990

First published 1990 by
Malthouse Press, Lagos, Nigeria

Reissue 2006
This edition published by Niyi Osundare

Distributed outside Africa by
African Books Collective, Oxford, UK
www.africanbookscollective.com

In North America:
Michigan State University Press, East Lansing
www.msupress.msu.edu

ISBN-10: 978-2601-40-3
ISBN-13: 978-978-2601-40-7

Printed by Lightning Source

For

Mahmud Modibo Tukur
&
John Oliver Killens

Whose dreams
in
form
our waiting laughters

I

Some laughters are very significant
- *(a line from Udje (Urhobo) song)*
(Courtesy Princess Adjija)

(flute and/or Clarinet; medley of voices)

I pluck these words from the lips of the wind
Ripe like a pendulous pledge;
Laughter's parable explodes in the groin
Of waking storms
Clamorous with a covenant
of wizened seeds

Tonalities. Redolent tonalities

Of wandering fancies yeasting into mirth,
Yeasting into glee in the crinkled lanes
Of giggling cheeks,
Lingering aroma of pungent chuckles,
The rave of ribs which spell the moments
In latitudes of tender bones

Tonalities. Redolent tonalities

I pluck these murmurs
From the laughter of the wind
The shrub's tangled tale
Plaited tree tops
And palms which drop their nuts

Like talents of golden vows
I listen solemnly to the banter
Of whistling fern
And I reap rustling rows
So fanatic in their pagan promise

Tonalities. Redolent tonalities

And laughing heels so fugitive
In the dust of fleeing truths

> Truth of the valley
> Truth of the mountain

> Truth of the boulder
> Truth of the river

> Truth of the flame
> Truth of the ash

> Truth of the sole
> Truth of the palm

> Truth of the sun
> Truth of the moon

> Truth of the liar
> Truth of the lair

> Truth of the castle
> Truth of the caste

> Truth of the desert
> Truth of the rain

Tonalities. Redolent tonalities

The rain. The rain
Truth of the rain's seven ingots
In the womb of the forge
And the seminal smoke which leaps
Above the roof, plodding skylanes
Before taunting thunder's raw temper
To a wild, unbridled deluge

3

The rain. The rain
The rain is *oníbánbántibá*
The rain is oníbànbàntibà*
The rain which taunts the roof's dusty laughter
In the comedy of February's unsure showers;
The wind is its wing, the lake
One liquid song in its fluent concert

Tonalities. Redolent tonalities

The wind has left springing laughter
In the loins of bristling deserts;
Sands giggle in grass,
Fallowing pebbles reach for sacks of scrotal pasture

Tonalities. Redolent tonalities

And still fugitive like a fairy,
The wind gallops like a thoroughbred
Dives like a dolphin
Soars into the waiting sky
Like *àwòdí*** with a beak of feathery oracles

Tonalities. Redolent tonalities

And laughing winds
So fugitive in
Our harried seasons
                    Who can tie
                    Them down with

---

* No specific semantic 'meaning'; used here as tonal counter-point
** Kite

4

                        The rope
of a single idiom   Who dare?

Tonalities. Redolent tonalities

Blame not, then,
The rapid eloquence of the running vowel
When words turn willing courier
In the courtyard of dodging ears
Can the syllable stall its tale
In impertinences of half-way fancies?

Tonalities. Redolent tonalities

I pluck these words
From the lips of running winds
When earth, yolk-yellow, clamours
For a warrant of wings
Tiptoe on the prudence of an anthill,
My covenant is clay,
Wisdom my silent wheel

Tonalities. Redolent tonalities

                    Wait
                          ing. . . .

          And the hours limp a-
          long,
          with
          band-
          ages
          of fractured moments

Every minute
heavy like an expectant rock,
the eyes labouring through
a century of winks
                    And the horse gallops
                    through an eternity of yawns
                    through the webbed wandering
                    of mangrove patience,
                    in the dusty mirror
                    which powders the broken mask
                    of swindled deserts

                    The horse gallops
                    through a street which stretches
                    like a rubbery code
                    before slipping a criminal disc
                    near the sacrum of the moon

                    Then the road narrows into artery
                    blossoms into egret dreams
                    which temper the whitened waiting

                          6

of showerless seasons

The road wanders into the street
the street wanders into the road
and road and street mellow into way,
lengthen into vision. . .

And the hours limp a-
long
longer than an April shower
longer than the cursive laughter of lightning
longer than the silk-cotton tree's mercy
in the loom of naked seasons
longer than the tortuous, broken queues
at the portals of Austerity factories!

Teach us the patience of the sand
which rocks the cradle of the river

Teach us the patience of the branch
which counts the seasons in dappled cropping

Teach us the patience of the rain
which eats the rock in toothless silence

Teach us the patience of the baobab
which tames the rage of orphaning storms

Teach us the patience of the cat
which grooms the thunder of leaping moment

Teach us, teach us, teach us. . . .

7

And the bitter-sweet clamour of initial beds
when dawn led me through the portals
of my first legs;
the swish of the hinge, the sticky wilderness
of reverent valleys
And my swollen pride, and her murmuring mercy,
the sepia helmet of stubborn tendons,
the concert of hips, the moistening motion
of oblivious moments. . . .

The wind was a song leaping through silky curtains,
through sonorous cric-cracs of shuttered windows
before hitting the street with a burst
of seminal silence.
The door was sentry,
the walls all ears. . . .

The deed was dawn
and we watched a tutored childhood
slip off in ripples of purple noons
Wisdom removed its veil, tucking it gently
in the belly of Time's uneasy shadows.

Moments borrow a heart
which pounds like tipsy elephants;
heelsounds struggle for names
on anonymous corridors,
and the door waits
for the fragrance of tender knocks

Seconds drag their feet
like lazy eons;
the clock jerks up both hands
like a felon spread-eagled
against a luminous wall

Waiting
>   for the heifer which bides its horns
>   in the womb of the calf

Waiting
>   for the nail which springs an ivory wonder
>   in the aprons of the finger

Waiting
>   for the tome which split its spine
>   in the spotted arena of reading eyes

Waiting
>   for the deer which loves its hide
>   and hunters who cuddle their flaying guns

Waiting
>   for the razor's stubbled glide
>   across the firmament of the beard

Waiting
>   for fists which find their aim
>   and idioms which split their atoms

>   in 'ploding shadows.

Waiting
>
> The anxious fumes of the visa awe-ffice
> thick with queries, thick with fear
> and stamps which bit trembling papers
> with purple fangs, and seals pompous
> like a mad phallus
>
> Narrow, the walls,
> high, imperiously white;
> the hangings stoke wondering dreams
> with their tourist havens;
> the future is one wavering complexion
> of the visaman's edict

Waiting
>
> in the visahouse is a chronicle of cold complaint:
> the calibrated aircon* coughs a chill
> in the sweaty calculations of a room
> aloud with doubt
> Exile, pilgrim, tripsters with feathered heels,
> there is a baggage of patience
> in the missionary temper of wanderlust.
>
>> The visaman, rightly suited,
>> his hair correct, his parting severe,
>> takes two furtive looks at the crowded hall
>> then shuts the window with a cold,
>> imperial hiss;

* Nigerian abbreviation for air-conditioner

11

The crowd's answer is a yawn,
and a few blank trips to a tired watch.

Passports are pass ports
The Atlantic is a wilderness of barbed walls
brooking no windows, its door of deafening
                                        steel
The key fell into spaceless water,
once upon a blue dragon,
then vanished, finally, into the shark's
intolerant belly.

Passports are pass ports
Knock still ye who may;
the Atlantic springs a door of deafening
                                        steel

And interrogation windows
And reluctant seats
And officers cold and clever

Like inquisitive godlings
And the metallic "No!"
And rapid ciphers
And repatriated dreams
And wingless fancies
And darkened noons. . . .

Knock still ye who may;
Seconds plod in leaden paces
in crowded visarooms.

Waiting
just waiting, the Custom's uniformed fingers
in the entrails of my puking box;
turning, turning, churning it like a bad diet,
probing for pellets, probing for dusts
prospecting for quiet little banks in the empire
of my bag;
and my bag, waiting, forbearing like a mule
turning every cheek;
still waiting while rugged fingers stretched me
full length against a rusty rule,
rattled the sacred shrub below my navel,

      Passports are pass ports
      Knock still ye who may
      the Atlantic springs a door of deafening steel

Waiting
>like the grass honing every blade
for the flesh of the dew

Waiting
>like the uncircumcised penis of okro
peeping out of the prepuce of dawn

Waiting
>like the lip of lettuce, the open palm of
*sokoyòkòtò**
beckoning the sky-bound shower, beckoning

Waiting
>like a raffia brush in the armpit of the valley,
iron straws on hips of dancing groves

Waiting
>like the beard for its chin, the knee for its cap
the night for its day, the prayer for its amen

Waiting
>like the forest for the umbrella of its mushroom
like the earth for the husband of its sky

Waiting
>like the tyrant for his noose.

---

* make-the-husband-robust: a favourite Nigerian vegetable.

14

Still waiting,
the drums, for the riot of the leg
leathery tales and answers bruised and bent
like the question-mark of the stick;
the stick, the stick, one Rumour of a tree,
itself the Rumour of a forest
where leaves only whisper their veins
and ferns strain their ribs, cheering,
just cheering, the tenor of reeling tales

Rumour is the sky's capacious fart
after one meal of delicious moons,
cinder left to wander
in the wake of talkative thunders

Rumour is the Pope's pimple, the monk's orgasm,
the muezzin's triumphal bark in the kennel of the night

Rumour is the wind which bides the echoes
of a floating truth.

Every comma has its period. . . .

like Rumour purring, catlike,
around the ears of the town,
gathering dust, gathering mud,
billowing here like a bison
narrowing there like a gnat
capsizing the gossip bowls of satellite whisperings
spiralling skywards like *igunnukò**
shrinking, shrinking, like the wizened memory
of an ageing sun

Still waiting,
Rumour slaps the tabloid face of ill-
literate mornings
bleeds screaming headlines like a noisy leech
spawns wondering gremlins in the hum
of lettery yards
before perching on the brow of every house
passed eave to eave like a prayerful song

Rumour is the faltering step of a practiced mask
the delicate gold of budding palm-fronds
the raffia tattle of thickening groves
where silence is silver
and shibboleths court the tongue
with ashen scabbards
Rumour is the regent of hush seasons
waiting for the second coming of assassinated Truths.

---

* a Yoruba masquerade popular for its shrinking-swelling
gymnastics.

Waiting
      like the tadpole in the crucible of the pond
      wriggling through mangrove traps
      dodging the fossil terror of rabid jaws
      capering with minnows,
      pulling the serpentine tails of fickle eels
      de-filing the watery fence of *Arogidigba**
      whose stomach is cemetery for hapless shoals

Just waiting
      for the tadpole's flowering into frog
      in the busy belly of indifferent waters
      Thus furnished with limb, furnished with leap,
      casting fertile beads like a pearly necklace
      around the isthmus of flooded seasons
      when frogtones are raucous baritones
      severely brown in ears of sinking eaves

Every tadpole is a frog-in-waiting
in the wasted waters of my greed en-tided land

---

* a mythical fish in D.O. Fagunwa's novel, notorious for its terror and greed.

17

Waiting
and the morning plucks its noon
and the moon, silver-aproned, waits
on the fertile greed of night,
dark-lamped, sweetened by the jolly tattle
of serenading birds, just dessert
of belching crickets

and the morning plucks its noon
January its April
while December stalks grey shadows
its beard askew with dust....

I am the testicle of the giant clock,
vane of the weathercock,
intangible grid of the shadow's millennial grid

I am the runic rithmetic of forgotten tribes
hearthy flame of the parrot's unquenching tale
blazing boulder of the Krakatoa
I am Death which kills itself for Life to be
the hours conspiring into days, wait

ing for festivals of birth,
for bleeding moons and seas scarlet with August
                                        spawning
for nectar, for pollen, for the mating hooves of
                          *ọlóbòunbọun**

---

* scarab beetle

18

for petals which reign and rot in the empire
of fragile forests
for water, for winds, for winds which bless distances
with wombs of scattering pods
for the whale which sperms the sea
for the seed which sires the season in caves
of sticky shadows
for days which brighten into nights, wait

ing for the reaper's shovel, glistening, glistening
in the mirror of the sun,
its handle of mortal wood,
its conquered ridges dull-red in the twilight
of wilting wails

Winnowing season: we-knowing-season
The chaff know their hell,
grains thresh a handsome pilgrimage
to the Jerusalem of the jaw;
and pumpkins unfold yellow peril
in the ripening ridges of compassionate suns

Winnowing season: we-knowing-season

"I am Croesus", quoth he,
waiting,
his breath a gail of gold,
his swagger varnished silver of a low intemperate sky

His head asks his crown
for a humble place in its gilded castle; ·
the crown pulls the head by its servile hair,
then leaves it hanging like an orphaned burden

Beyond Reason, beyond Necessity
beyond Distribution which tames the Excess
of uneven mountains
beyond Virtue, beyond Need
beyond Truth which straightens the serpent
of stammering jungles
Croesus heaves a glittering crown on his head,
his neck shortening like a senile cricket's

Beyond Reason, beyond Necessity
in the orgy of crimson claws
which darken the rainbow of striving ribs

in the belly of the goblet where murdered grapes
sip their scarlet wails,
the moon, the moon, is up;
the sceptre barks its canine edict
castles crash, mortally tired of their medieval legs
waters breaking, waters breaking
royal fishes smell purple twilight
in the cemetery of baking sands

Waiting

     like the Bastille, for the screaming stones
     of turbulent streets;
     their bread is stone
     their dessert garnished sand from the kitchen
     of hearthless seasons
     And when the humble axe finally heeds its
                             noble task,
     the head descends, lumpen dust in its royal
                                mouth

     Behold the wonder;
     the crown is only a cap!

        Òrògòdodo Òrògòdo
        Òrògòdodo Òrògòdo
        Ọbá bá ti béyì
        Ó mò d'Òrògòdòdo o o o o*

        The king's brave legs are bone and flesh
        Bone and flesh, bone and flesh
        The king's brave legs are bone and flesh
        The castle is a house of mortar and stone
        Mortar and stone, mortar and stone
        A chair is wood which becomes a throne

---

* Òrògòdòdo Òrògòdo
A king who dances with a dizzy swing
Orògòdo straight he goes.

(Òrògòdo in Ikere mythology is a remote place of banishment for
dishonourable rulers)

And Croesus builds a castle of strident stone.
Oh teach us the patience of the Rain
which eats the rock in toothless silence

Waiting, still waiting,
>Like soldier-ants routing fat cockroaches
>in columns of lengthy fury
>
>Like a hatching fruit peeping at the sun
>between the rasping duel of jealous leaves
>
>Like the river lisping long vowels in the pro-
>tracted dialogue of restless valleys
>
>Like mountains unmasking mists, and hillsteps
>heavy in the armpit of sprawling shadows
>
>Like termites vying valiantly, vying valiantly
>with the dark valour of iron wood
>
>Like the sword growing too large
>for its sheath
>
>Like the sun seeing red in sunset skies, and
>grand oracles washing hands in changing tides

Waiting
>   on the stairs of the moon
>   creaking up and down
>   the milkyways of fastidious comets
>   bled into speed, plucked off the vortex
>   of falling flares
>   my foot knows the timbre of fiery skies
>   where songs still dripping
>   with the sap of the wind
>   dry their limbs in furnaces
>   of baking proverbs
>
>   My song is space
>   beyond wails, beyond walls
>   beyond insular hieroglyphs
>   which crave the crest
>   of printed waves.

My song is the even rib
in the feather of the soaring bird
the pungent salt and smell of
earth
where seeds rot for roots to rise

My song is the root
touching other roots
in a covenant below the crust
beyond the roving camera of the eye

My song is the embryo of day
in the globule of the rising dew;
a vow which earths the Word
in regions of answerable rains

My song is ògbìgbòtirigbò*
waiting on the stairs of the moon
garnering lights, garnering shadows,
waiting

_____

*a large bird which flies high in the sky.

Laughters, waiting laughters
                peals of silence

            thunder of rocking teeth

            bolts of syncopated seas

            shifting continent of the cheek

            musing estuary of the jaws

            incandescent contour of the brows

            batting array of retreating eyes

            spreading escapade of seeing lips

            echoing, echoing cascade of scarlet caves.

II

*The freedom of any society varies proportionately
with the volume of its laughter*
— Zero Mostel

(kora and/or goje; medley of voices)

Wait
       ing

And the hours limp a-
long
with
band-
ages
of fractured moments

Waiting

like a felon yoked to a tryst with the noose,
a groom for the magic of the bridal night
a husband pacing the scented corridors of the labour
                                                    ward
a home-sick traveller on the platform of tardy trains
a big-bellied billionaire for the aroma of Rhine-rouge
                                               champagne
a deer so conscious of the legend of the gun
a coup-drunk battalion for the bugles of power-ful
                                                   dawns
a termite-eaten thatch for the advent of the rain
a waiter
a waited-upon

Time
       ambles
in

         diverse
paces
         with
diverse
         persons

The Atlantic
                picks its teeth
with shrapnels
                of sepia bones
crowns every dinner
                with goblets of crimson groans
before going to bed
                on skeins of spidered twilight

The Criss and cross rails

in a crisis of sleep
ing
                    steel

Only savage rust
threatens the knots
with a tooth of filed water

And when millipede legs un
do the distance
on spines of serpentine columns

the evening explodes
with a diesel rigour
in its coughing horns.

No matter how fast
the millipede may run
will it not always find the earth ahead

Waiting?

And the cry
is deeper than the wound

lodged in the spine
of swindled mountains

knowing its fire
unblinking its ice

spelling the purple hilt
of ruling swords

The cry, oh the cry
is deeper than the wound

The axe-man
      came

     saw
and nearly

      conquered....

The cry is
  deeper than
    the wo
     und

(for the 10th of January)

Still waiting
like the wound for its scar
the cruel kindness of surgical knives
ripping yellow skulls like a sword fish through
the mangrove of waiting waters.

The nerves have gone to bed;
gone utterly out in the sway of ethering nights,
the moon here is one white ceiling, un-
forgetably white;
stars hoard their glitter in the blinkless socket
of staring walls;
there are no trees here;
the knifeman's green toga is ambush for red stabbings

All the world is a canvas,
island of scarlet seas,
(in) continent splash of prentice painters

I have seen fright, seen fire
I have seen the truth of the lie

I am an egret
red with the storm of bleeding seasons,
tabled, sewn up, like the hapless toad
of a sophomore science. . . .

I, too, have witnessed the pasture
in the purple bleatings of probing knives

35

And   minutes
drag   their

feet   so
in-   finitely

in   grey
boots   of

leaden   hours
each   wink
a   wail

each   wail
one   eon

in   the
sleepy   chronology

of   drastic
          etherings

Time ambles in diverse paces. . . .

The innocence of the Niger
waiting, waiting
fourhundredseasons
for the proof of the prow
waiting
for the irreverent probing of pale paddles
waiting
for the dispossessing twang of alien accents
                                        waiting
for scrolls of serfdom, hieroglyphs of calculated
                                        treacheries
waiting
withoutafacewithoutanamewithoutafacewithouta-
waiting
for the Atlantic which drains the mountains with
                                        practiced venom
waiting
for a history which snails towards the coast,
a delta of meandering dreams
waiting
for the bubbles of Bussa
where rock riles river and a conquering boat
fathoms the sand in a tumble of mysty furies
waiting
the Nile knows, the Limpopo lingers,
the Kilimanjaro preserves the lore in icy memory
waiting
        But for how long can the hen wait
        Whose lay is forage for galloping wolves?

Ask Sharpeville
ask Langa

ask Soweto

Where green graves cluster like question marks

Ask Steve
ask Walter
ask Nelson

who seed waiting moments with sinews of fleeting
seasons

Ask
the metaphor of our strength

Ask
the strength of our metaphor

Ask
the breaking, broken stones of Robbing Island
where the ocean's water is sulphur
where aching walls harbour a dragon
in every crack

Ask
the bleeding anthem on the lips of wounded kraals

Ask
the dappled darings on billowing banners

Dappled
like the grave where Sankara lies, a waiting eagle,

Dappled
like the windward dream of Bishop

Dappled
   like the seeing History of Rodney

Ask:
   the stone under Nelson's hammer is bread
   river with faithful wings
   wind with jasmine in its breath;

Ask
   the stone is an ocean
   which cannot count its shoal of eyes

Waiting
   for the kaffir buried four hundred days a year
   in orphaning pits
   for the Boer trapped by the diamond dazzle
   of unanswerable plunderings

Time ambles in diverse paces. . .

Waiting
like the crusty verb of a borrowed tongue
salty with the insult of the sea
its nouns dotted with little maps
its proverbs crimson with memories of conquering
waves
Here, my tongue
But where, the mouth?

The tongue is parrot
Of another forest

Couched and caged
In a strident silence

Fed the seeds
of an alien tree

Routed by its root
Logged by its stem

A white white tongue
In a black black mouth

Here, my mouth
But where, the tongue?

And the tongue hangs out its blade,
blunted
by the labyrinthine syntax of ghostly histories

In the lore of the larynx,
in the velar enclave of orphaned probings,
Thoughts draw battle lines with Words
and the wind is loud with the deafening tower
of pidgin babels.

History's stammerer,
when will this tongue, uprooted, settle back
in the pink peat of the mouth

History's stammerer,
when will this wandering tree seek
the loam of its father's forest

History's stammerer
when will your memory master
the vowels of your father's name?

Time ambles in diverse paces ...

With all the oceans
        in the fountain of their pen

they scribble
        Earth's history

on the back
        of a postage stamp

Infections like a yawn
the moon staggers out of
the kitchen of night,
the skylanes littered with pots
of broken shadows

From the ruptured slumber of the stars
from the begging banter of the dew
which ekes a fragile peace
from the riot of rainless seasons,
Earth sprawls like a famished bull-

waiting for its horn of rain.

III

Lofty sorrows cast shadows of lengthy laughters

(gangan, bata, ibembe in varying accents;
medley of voices)

Waiting,
all ways waiting,
like the mouth for its tongue

My land lies supine
like a giant in the sun
its mind a slab of petrified musing
its heart a deserted barn
of husky cravings

And in this March,
this March of my heated coming,
the sky is high in the centre of the sun
cobs faint in the loins of searing stalks,
the tuber has lost its voice in the stifling womb
of shrivelled heaps

A king there is
in this purple epoch of my unhappy land;
his first name is Hunger,
his proud father is Death
Which guards the bones at every door

And the vultures are fat
crows call a feast at every dusk;
markets wear their stalls like creaking ribs
the squares are sour with the absence
of friendly feet

And Fat Cows swallow Lean Cows
and the Pharaoh who umpires the orgy

45

on the bank of a sniggering Niger
has neither wit nor will to wave a royal wand
The sages say his own cupboard groans
with a caché of glittering bones;

Just how can a soiled finger
clean its stymied brothers?

Ordinances tumble down like iron showers
decrees strut the streets like swaggering emperors
hangmen hug the noose like a delicate baby
and those who die thank Death
for his infinite mercies

Ìbòsí ò!*
Hands which go mouthwards
in seasons of ripening corn
have lost their homeward trip
to the waiting bowl

And yet corpulent towncriers
clog the ears of listless lanes;
praise-singers borrow the larynx
of eunuch thunders

The Desert marches in from the North;
the Sea sneaks in from the South;
manacles on their right,
on their left, chains recently oiled
with barrels of ancient treasons ...

 Waiting.
_____
*A loud cry for help

My land is a desert
waiting for the seminal fury
of uneasy showers,

Waiting,
            like the corpulent clergy
                    for his tithes

like the white-wigged judge
            for his turkey

like the hard-faced don
            for his chair

like the policeman
            for his bribe

    waiting.

Waiting
still waiting,
like the strident summon of hasty edicts,
bellowed by the smoking lips of vulgar guns,
signed in blood, unleashed in the crimson spine
of trembling streets

And the winds return,
laden with adamantine thou-shalt-nots
of green gods;
a jointless Fear goosesteps the compound of our minds
with epaulettes of night, belts of fuming cobras;
purple swaggers manacle our days
and trees swap their fruits for stony orders

    These are seasons of barking guns
    These are seasons of barking guns;
    They whose ears are close to the earth
    Let them take cover in the bunker of their wits

The lion grows iron-maned and bans the flock
The crocodile turns stone-jawed and bans the shoals

The cloud grows cotton-headed and bans the rain
The valley turns tunnel-hearted and bans the river

The sky grows swollen-headed and bans the sun
The sea turns beady-eyed and bans its salt

The shogun grows cannon-drunk and bans himself

But are these the messiahs
who came four seasons ago
with joyful drums and retinues of chanted pledges?
Where now the aura,
where, the anointed covenant of eloquent knights?

II

And bellowed the shogun
with a swaggering viper in his armpit,
a raging geyser in his regimented nose
Bellowed the shogun
with a dusky grain around his lips:

        I proscribe   the snail
        I proscribe   the shell

        I proscribe   the frog
        I proscribe   the tadpole

        I proscribe   the sea
        I proscribe   the sky

        I proscribe   the sun
        I proscribe   the moon

        I proscribe   the tale
        I proscribe   the TRUTH

        I proscribe   HISTORY!

III

The bison who thinks he is the king of the wild

        let him remember raging elephants
            with legs of mortar

The hillock which thinks it is the frontier of heights
            let it remember the Kilimanjaro so hot
                with a peak of simmering snow

The streamlet which thinks it is the Zambesi of the lore
            let it remember the sea merges earth
                and sky in realms of misty blue

The prophet who thinks he has conquered tomorrow
            let him mount galloping mountains and marvel
                dodging canters of the horse of time

The shogun who says he is an awesome god
            let him take note of burning statues
                and streets wild with vengeful spears...

IV

And waiting,
still waiting,
like the mouth for its fiery tongue.

Waiting

    like the pothole for its po(r)tion of blood

    like the smart General for his umpteenth million

    like idle bugs for their nightly feast

    like the prattling tongues of parliaments of ruse

    like Blaise for a trusting Thomas

    like Imelda for her shoes.

And seasons which wax so loud
with the eloquence of the sword
arrogant thrusts and chronicles of desperate gorings

Blind steel, unfalteringly deaf the blade's hunger
when wounded winds bemoan their gashes
and grasses bow under their crimson yoke,

astonished beyond recounting

The mountains are their saddles
scurrying hills footholds for their grating gallops;
their leaps are lethal, gales fan their ancient rage.

Oh red memory of hopping scabbards,
crusading Knights, east-eyed Saracenes
in turbans of whirling skulls

The sword here is not mightier than the pen;
the sword is the pen running red rubrics
on the fragile page of cardboard memories

     Genesis of the trigger
     Fate-ful exodus of prisoned bullets;
     Iron gospels bend the lectern of preaching pistols

     The plough has no share in
     the malady of running swords;
     only hungry hatchets, rapiers of ravishing fury

Oh red, so red,
the bark of cannibal guns
waiting, for the after-silence of pacific twilights.

Waiting
     like a hyena
     for the anniversary of its pounce;
     waiting
     like an African despot
     for the seventieth year of his rule.

And the multitudes waiting,
all ways waiting,
in the corridors of hungry shadows

stretched skeletally out
in rice queues, bread queues
salt queues, water queues

long like a scarlet tear;
from the short-tempered scourge
of the winkless sun

to the sprawling terror
of twilights of chilly hearths
an emptiness balloons the stomach,

lethal like a blinding plague,

How many fishes will quell the rage
of this political hunger,
how many loaves?

The messiahs peep at
the tattered hordes from the paradise
of a Mercedesed distance

Their fences are high
their gates wild with
howls of alsatian soldiery

They too are waiting

for questions which find answers
at the back of History's book.

Waiting,
>like Hitler in his bunker
>like Marcos in Hawaii
>like Idi Amin in a sandy purgatory

>The lizard's waiting custom
>is a chronicle of nods;
>the pig bares its mind
>in a century of hum-hums

>I saw *alápàndàgi** surging gleefully
>in the corridors of the lake;
>one frightful hook later
>it lay surprised at the bottom
>of a boiling pot

>the hapless fish knew too late
>the mortal ambiguity of water

Verily, verily
as the roof is the crown-
ing glory of the house,

Every day has its dog
Every dog must have its day.

---

* a fish of the tilapia family.

Waiting
just waiting
like the praying lamb
for the saviour of a lion.

Have you seen Àdùfé in the waiting moon,
Have you seen her fins and tail
Of dazzle-new scales?

Àdùfé had a dip
In the stream between the hills
Where the bank is clay,
Kneaded into golden patterns
By the calling feet of star-entangled mountains,
Where sands have no secret
In the simple clarity of blushing fountains

Àdùfé had a dip

And every shrub became
A kitchen of soap,
Every tree stretched out
A basket of sponge.
The noonday sun was ready towel
The wind waited in the wing
Like a loquacious robe

And the foamy touch of soap
On her brow became the laughter
Of the clouds,
The shy globules on her cheek
Were a quarry of delicious diamond
The pebbles broke into song,
Provoked by the velvety warmth
Of her guiless soles

Shadows peeped behind the mountains;
The sun stood still in its wondering sky

Àdùfé's dialogue with the river
Was a saga of careful whispers;
First, her leg
Then, her arm
Then, the eloquent valley which loomed
Between her upright breasts

She swayed, she swam
She patted the cheeks of the laughing stream.
Wild with joy, clean like a mint,
She climbed back to the bank,
Back to her waiting clothes;
And just then she saw
The memorable gift of the wonderful river:

> Her lower side was now a tail
> of silvery scales.

My tale is a ripening kola
Waiting
For the golden teeth of mellowing seasons.

(For NLC88, and the Generals)

Says the hyena to a clan of lambs:

> "Today, I dissolve your flock
> For making such loud noises
> About my eating habits.
>
> I will now set up a group
> To select your spokemen
> Who will come freely to my den
> With your woes and sundry views"

Òkerebú kerebú
Kerebú kerebù

And the snake says to the toad;
"I have not had a meal
For a good one week;
And my stomach yearns
For your juicy meat"

"Suppose I turn into a mountain?"
Asks the toad,

"I will level you in the valley
Of my belly"

"Suppose I turn into a river?"

"You will flow easily through
The channels of my mouth"

"Suppose I become one
Of your favourable children?"

"I will eat you
With all the motherly love
In this world"

The toad then turns into a rock
And the snake swallows it
With delicious despatch

Ah! àràmòndà*
The mouth has swallowed something
Too hard for the mill of the stomach

Òkerebú kerebú
Kerebú kerebù

Our tale is a bride
Waiting
For the nimble fancy of the grooming ear.

---

* Wonder of wonders!

Bi bi bi bi bi bi bi

Bi a a a a

Let the foot grow wary
Of the caverns of the shoe

Let the cockroach beware
Of the dance of the hen

The rain which fell the other day
Its drops were pecked dry
By roosters of the golden pen

I am no teller of foul tales
Watch my lips
I am no teller of foul tales

My eagle is a nestling
Waiting, still waiting
For its fable of feathers

Bi bi bi bi bi bi bi

Bi a a a a!

Sky-high domes
Incontinent bells:
      My country is a prayer
      Waiting
      For a distant amen.

Omí i ́ lo o, iyanrìn loòkún ródè
Omi i lo o, iyanrin lookun rode
Aye mo ré ́dè, e emee jémí lo lóona o o o*

Even when the horse has galloped home
Galloped finally home on the spur of sweating dusks
Roadside shrubs hold on to their legacy of dust
The tracks are red with alphabets of passing hoofs

Aye mo ro de, e mee jemi lo loona o

Even when elephants plod through
Our ripening farms
When stalks are sad
And broken buds lament their bleeding scars,
A few flowers cling, still,
To the beard of the valley
Dancing, dancing, in the whistling wind

Aye mo ro de, e mee jemi lo loona o

We are a village of hills,
A village of rolling hills,
Those who sharpen dark knives
For our fledgeling voice
Will go back home, drowned in the deluge
Of its echoes
Of its echoes
Of its echoes
In the deluge of its stubborn e. . .ch. . .o. . .es

Aye mo ro de, e mee jemi lo loona o o

The water is going
Going going going
The water is going

---

* The last two stanzas of this poem are a mediated translation of
this Ikere song.

But the sea waits, still
On the silence of the sand
The water is going

I wait for life
And that is why my heels are strong

Chuckling jungles
Impertinent tales. . .
How can a frightened flock
Mine the awe
Of the hyena's metallic

Laughter?

Waiting
      like the yam for the knife. . .

My tongue has not stumbled
Upon the outcrop of hidden words

My tongue has not stumbled

I have not told a bulbous tale
In the presence of *asopa**

I have not shouted "Nine!"
In the backyard of the one with a missing finger

Ah my tongue has not stumbled

Everyone knows
I have never asked the toad
Any story about missing tails

Nor pestered the sportly bat for its head-
Down sleep in the acrobatics of clumsy nights

The world's trap is waiting, always waiting,
For the unwary rodent

But if the knife waits all seasons
For the yam

---

* one with swollen scrotum

Should the yam also wait
For the hoofs of the knife?

A baby antelope
Once asked her pensive mother:
    Tell me, mother
    How does one count the teeth
    Of a laughing lion?

They will kill many moons
On the saddle of their heels
They who stalk our banks
For snores of slumbering crabs*

They will stretch many seasons
In the mid-day night of distant groves
They who strive to flout the face
Behind our prizest mask.

Down down the earth
Is the whisper of stirring roots
Down in the ocean's darkest womb
*Oremodo*** garners in its protean eggs

The bird weaves its song
Across the paradise of the sky
The plantain fans the wind
With the elephant ears of its leaves

They who will prison the whirlwind
Let them build their fancies of fair stone
They who hope to chain the sun
Let them build a forge of frigid fire.

---

* There is a Yoruba belief that crabs never sleep
** a small mythical fish extraordinarily active and fertile

The feet I see are waiting for shoes
The sores are waiting for an urge-nt balm

The stomachs in the streets are waiting for coming
harvests
Water-pots are waiting in famished homesteads.

The loom I see is naked as a nail
The rags are a commonwealth of lice

The faces I see are a mask of wrinkles
The voices wounded by a battalion of edicts

The gods I see carry a clay foot in every slipper
The acolytes wear a veil of flammable straw

The eyes I see are waiting for rallying visions
The fists for a bolt of implacable thunder

For time it may take
Time it may take.

The stammerer wil one day call his
Fa-fa-fa-ther-ther's na-na-na-me!

Waiting
       like the eternal wisdom of
       Mosáféjó*
       who gave one daughter
       in marriage to six suitors

----

* I-am-averse-to-litigations.

IV

Correct your laughter
— *Tchicaya U Tam'si*

*(flute, kora, gangan, sekere;
voices in final flourish)*

Waiting
      like the silver fire of the adze, tongue honed
      on the eloquence of the wind,
      sphere of the Sphinx, menopause of
                    Menomotapa
      chipping shapes whose destiny defines our
                       wake
      and the truth of the tension which dwells
      the tabernacles of gathering biceps. Wait-
      ing, the adze, a question-mark seeking
      urgent answers from the hew of the hulk,
      fashioning fairies from the fancy of lying
                    trunks,
      sermons from stones, books from rune-y
                    woods
      chipping and shaping, chipping and shaping,
      making big dreams small for bigger dreams

               *

      like the drum for the universe of the palm,
      of yawning knuckles green with the dawn of
                    the grove,
      of the telegraph of the hide, wired in purple
      throbbings and syllables of echoing chambers,
      of idioms swollen with the legend of the voice,
      and legs which learn their lines in
      the orchestra of dusted crossings

               *

Lean lines, fat lines
intrepid strokes which strike the canvas
like venturing streets,
where moons are pale with trekking
and stars plod the sky like diamond tips.
Lanes borrow luminous breaths from the
                                    largesse
of stringent brushes,
houses are only a hint, dotted here and there
by the oblivion of hazy hues; back-
grounded, the sea is a misty promise;
Trees learn their name from shadows
of sleeping lakes

Red
is the drivelling chatter of the watermelon
Brown
lends a hump from the (s) table of baking seasons
Yellow
yelps like a yoyo, before finally chasing its
Green
to the tree of Easter mangoes
my daubster merely whispers his royal
Blue
and the canvas turns a sea of princely dolphins

A luminous intimation leaps off the trestle,
breaks through the barricade of the board,
before joining the sky in the fringes of the canvas,

drizzling indigo, in the tenor of Negro songs,
drizzling indigo, in the immortal basin of the dyeing
                                    hand

drizzling indigo, in the clever pupil of the Caucasian
eye
drizzling indigo, in the sapphire wail of Oppenheimer's
pitdoms
drizzling indigo, in the shadowy bend of fledgeling
laughters

waiting

(in flight• Amsterdam-Lagos, 4-4-88)

Hungry as the sea
hungry as the blue belly of its foaming tantrums
salt in their blood, running iodine in the goitre
of craning isthmus, intemperate pressure
in the capillary of the waves

billowing, all ways billowing, like a frantic flag
a galloping school of camels with their humps of mist
hooves of liquid depths, caravans of furious shoals.
The sea's memory here is an infirmary of eels
where echoes slip like mucous whispers

and a shell-shocked silence garners the splinters
like a harvest of strafing falcons. And the shells,
relieved of their fleshy burden, whistle celibate fancies
in the monastery of bony chambers. A silent thunder
                                rules
the firmament of the waves. A silent thunder

so innocent of the rumble of the tide. For the sea,
too, is silence of seeing sands, silence of unspoken
                                bones...
The sea is silence. But silence is not the sea,
so white, so wild with whiskers of buried jaws;
worsted galleons, stigma of manacled crossings.

Seven tongues has the sea, a tribe of roaring accents:
the Atlantic which swaggers in cant and cannon,
the Pacific which maims the peace in scarlet seasons
another sea, red still, with the cemetery of galloping
                                Pharaohs

the Mediterranean foams at the edge of its moderate
                                                    mouth. . .

My history is a mountain drained by thirsty oceans,
my chronicle's coast is a delta of fractured fingers

Waiting
         still
              waiting

for the laughing rainbow on the brow of the mist
when sea meets sky on a canvas of colour-ful suns.

Whoever hasn't kissed the sticky lips
of an envelope,
licked the glossy spine of a stamp,
lacing pigeon winds with syllables
of feathered breaths

Whoever hasn't fondled the legend of the grape
teased the mammary temper of the joyous pawpaw
incited humble carrots to riot,
swollen with the pink bluff
of February's relentless sun

Whoever hasn't trampled the wound of the road
touched sour streets on their bruised elbow
mopped the copper sore of August

Whoever hasn't touched the armpit of the rock
watched care-less boulders tremble
with potent laughter
savoured the jubilant tears of lilting lava

Whoever hasn't seen a caravan of Ways
racing after their dashing Means. . .

Whoever hasn't,

is still waiting.

Our countless vulnerabilities
the breasts of our forests done bare by the Treachery
of the wind
The travail of our trees skinned by the howling razor
Of indifferent gales,
The lymph of the leaves, of stalks stoking earth's pity
With running scars of unceremonious sunderings;
The baobab's beauty is deep in the salon of the soil;
There is a scorching terror in the spectacle of bleeding
roots.

Countless vulnerabilities
Of the fragile truth beneath the swaggering snake
Far from flaming fangs and scales of silvered steel
Far from the buried shrapnel waiting like a stalking paw
At the back of roaring mountains;
How can the cobra cross the valley without gliding
On the hidden blades of tricky terrains?

Countless vulnerabilities
And ticking tremors in the breast of sleeping mountains
The uncertain diet in the stomach of the night
Genuflections in the temples of last rains,
Of the tongue turning cactus in the desert of the mouth

Countless vulner-abilities

And the strength of our fear
Waiting, tail over head,
For the fear of our strength.

Long-
er
than
the
y
a
w
n
of
the
moon
in
a
sky
so
brown
with
heels
of
fleeting
fancies
a
diamond
tear
waits,
tremulous,
in
the
eye
of
the
cloud,
dropping

dropping
dropping
later
in
hails
of
greening
showers,
tendrils
dance
their
joy,
the
heaps
are
drums
of
kicking
vows
waiting
waiting
waiting
for
pageants
of
rain-bow
harvest

Sometimes
the early sun lies limbless
in the ambush of unkindly clouds;
an opening day meets waking moments
with a cavalry of iron groans

Sometimes
joy-killers reach for the neck
of our laughter,
dragging through sweat-soaked dusks
the memory of our mirth

then tilt their ears
to the purple horn of running wails,
reaping strident guffaws
from travails of martyred whimpers

Yes, they strip our distance runners
of the beauty of their legs,
then throw our champion fish
into the wilderness of the sea,
dispossessed of its sturdy fins

Sometimes

But the sun strides through the clouds
to the threshold of noon,
strong, untrappably wiser;
a quiet smile informs the sky's diurnal face
and the cloud's sullen brow
is promise of a gentle shower

Joy-killers will find ready grave
in the labyrinth of their venom

Laughter will surely come back
to the paradise of our lips

(sowing)

And when a long-awaited shower
has rid earth's brow
of the debris of sweltering seasons

When heavy clouds have known
their labour, and a steel-handed sun
midwives the mists

in noons of convectional brewings,
rivers learn once more
their liquid lessons, the valley so

       quick with veins of fresh tiding

When a long-awaited shower
has softened the pilgrimage of the dibble,
corn-grains sing their way to germinal roots

of lying ridges. Seedlings dream truant tendrils
in the moistening bed of unpunctual heaps;
the tuber is one patience away,

climbing through stakes
through pinna-leafed groves
through vines which twine the moons

       like wayward pythons

Bent now
the farmer's back;
the hoe's edict chills the spine

of sowing seasons. And the sweat
which rivers down the mountain of the brow,
finds gathering basin at the root of coming harvests

Oh seminal seasons
oh moons of sporing shadows;
laughing barns are just a tear away

and the plenitude which threshes the throes of
                              ripening valleys

And the hunchback flings a look
at the reeling vista of recurring History;
the sanguinary passion of slaving sagas,
the rusty anthem of the chain;
and dawn's own children breaking bread
with rats in streets without names, without light...

And the conquistador's severe coming,
his hoof of iron,
and the dialect of the gun
the staccato syntax of treacherous treaties
and the fires of Adowah
and the race to Fashoda
and the sea red every drop with vessels
of ruptured hearts
and Africa quartered like a giant mango
on the haggling stretch of Berlin tables

> When will every serf know his lord,
> every bicep its fleecing whip?

And the sages say to the hunchback:
how crooked your burden, how unsightly!
And the hunchback reels out a rapid answer:
the mountain which surmounts my chest
has its roots in the regions below my knees

Whoever seeks the anguish of the river
let him ask the oracle of distant mountains

*

And the eunuch returns, trailed every step
by offsprings of forgotten dreams,
and the cripple stands blissfully tall
on his abandoned legs

    The bushfowl hatches its eggs far, very far, from
    the clever fingers of the foraging hunter

And the desert returns with a pasture of pliant shepherds

and trampled dust is wizened clay
in dawns of moulding breaths

    The earthworm knows the route
    of trampling warriors

And the tempest returns, a petal of whispering bliss
in its shriven hand
and the shogun's last whimper is alpha
of re-tiring triggers

    *Wèrèpè** spells out its freedom
    in a rampart of stinging needles

And the bat surprises blazing noons
with the brilliance of hidden eyes;
and the donkey finds a cure for its deadly patience

    The sun unmasks its name
    in a running lane of fugitive shadows.

---

* cow-itch (a plant "with spicular hairs on the fruits penetrating into one's skin
causing irritation" – A.C. Abraham, *Dictionary of Modern Yoruba*

Waiting,
       still waiting

like the brown fable of rainless regions,
the sun's stony victory in the wilderness
of fleeing dust

the arid lament of trees without leaves
without songs
the baobab's missionary patience

and rivers whose beds know no liquid snore
in a season of slumbering moons; cracked,
the lips of voiceless grass

the melon's bulbous legend is a lie
of shrivelled rinds; noonglares hang
heavy with the tang of fermenting cassava

water-holes are receding sockets
in the distant eye of dazzling earth;
every path knows now the pilgrim –

age of gaping pots

only edicts come down, in metallic deluge,
from cloudy chambers of rumbling guns,
the fields wet with the invisible blood

of assassinated dreams

waiting, then, like Masekela's eternal song*
waiting,
for the green fingers of laughing showers

_____

*'Waiting for the Rain'

What happens to the tendril which waits too long
In the furnace of the sun

What happens to the song which waits too long
In the labyrinth of the throat

What happens to the prayer which waits too long
Without an amen

What happens to the face which waits too long
Without the memory of a mask

What happens to LAUGHTER which waits too long
In the compost of anguished seasons?

What.....?

Waiting
still waiting

Grant us

the fortitude of the lamb which lames a lion-
without inheriting its claws

the daring of the egg which hardens its temple
in a golgotha of breaking shells

the valour of the abyss which hurls its crest
above the conspiracy of severe mountains

the wisdom of seasons which see
the hidden dagger in a plumage of smiles

Grant us

the depth of the sky, height of the sea
fancies which flesh the bones of grating facts

moons which dwell the sky of every brow
on nights when love's labour is never lost.

I pluck these words from the laughter of the wind:
The liquid breath of the Monsoon's millennial riddle,

Breezy nights so civil with the etiquette of restless stars
The penetrating sympathy of harmattan dawns.

From the polyglot hurricane of nights of easy carnage
Waiting moments distill banners of purple peace

From the fugitive slumber of seasons of chloroform
fancy
Waiting moments brew a sentry of vigilant wisdom

> For so elephantine have grown the heels
> These several ages of anonymous waiting....

It is the scabbard which knows the name of the sword
It is the sky which smells footsteps of passing moons

Laughter it is
Which knows the name of hidden mouths.

Our laughter these several seasons is the simper-
Ing sadness of the ox which adores its yoke,

The toothless guffaw of empty thunders
In epochs of unnatural drought

The season calls for the lyric of other laughters

> New chicks breaking the fragile tyranny
> Of hallowed shells

A million fists, up,
In the glaring face of complacent skies

A matchet waiting, waiting
In the whetting shadows of stubborn shrubs

A boil, time-tempered,
About to burst.

CPSIA information can be obtained at www.ICGtesting.com
Printed in the USA
LVOW080813060912

297619LV00001B/68/A